Landforms

Developed at
Lawrence Hall of Science
University of California at Berkeley

Published and Distributed by **Delta Education**

ISBN 1-58356-848-4
542-2018

4 5 6 7 8 9 10 QUE 09 08 07 06 05

TABLE OF CONTENTS

MAPS AND HOW THEY ARE MADE

Most people are familiar with maps. We use *transit,* or road, maps when we travel from one place to another. We see weather maps on the evening news. A map of a sports stadium or concert hall tells us where to find our seats. A map of the United States can help us locate places where important events occur or where people live. A map is simply a picture of an area, usually a part of the Earth's surface. Most maps are drawn from a bird's-eye view. They show the Earth as if it were being looked down upon from above.

SCALES AND SYMBOLS

Maps are drawn to *scale.* That means that a small distance on a map equals a larger distance in the real world. For example, 1 centimeter on a map might equal 1 kilometer in an actual place. Map scales are usually shown as ratios or fractions such as 1:100 or 1/100. A map's scale is used to measure the distance between two places on the map. Then it is translated into the actual distance between the two places. For example, think of two cities 5 centimeters apart on a map. The map has a scale in which 1 centimeter equals 1 kilometer. This means the two cities are actually 5 kilometers (3 miles) apart in the real world. A large-scale map shows a small land area in more detail. A small-scale map 3hows a larger area in less detail. A city street map's scale might have 1 centimeter equal to 250 meters (0.4 inches equal to 825 feet). The scale of a map of the entire Earth might have 1 centimeter equal to 500 kilometers (0.4 inches equal to 300 miles). A map's scale is often printed near the margin of the map.

Another type of map scale is the *graphic scale.* Graphic scales look like small rulers. They are also usually found in the margins of maps. To use a graphic scale, place the edge of a sheet of paper between two places on the map. Mark the distance between the places on the edge of the paper. Then lay the paper along the graphic scale to find out

A map scale

SCALE 1:25 000

```
30'        '01              '02              '03      10'
1                                                        1 MILE
   1000   0   1000  2000  3000  4000  5000  6000  7000 FEET

   1          .5          0                        1 KILOMETER
```

CONTOUR INTERVAL 10 FEET
DATUM IS MEAN SEA LEVEL
DEPTH CURVES AND SOUNDINGS IN FEET—DATUM IS MEAN LOW WATER
SHORELINE SHOWN REPRESENTS THE APPROXIMATE LINE OF MEAN HIGH WATER
THE MEAN RANGE OF TIDE IS APPROXIMATELY 9 FEET

SURFACE FEATURES

Levee	————	*Levee*
Sand or mud area, dunes, or shifting sand		*Sand*
Intricate surface area		*Strip Mine*
Gravel beach or glacial moraine		*Gravel*
Tailings pond		*Tailings Pond*

MINES AND CAVES

Quarry or open pit mine	⚒
Gravel, sand, clay, or borrow pit	⚒
Mine tunnel or cave entrance	⤙
Prospect; mine shaft	X ◼
Mine dump	*Mine dump*
Tailings	*Tailings*

A map legend from the United States Geological Survey (USGS)

what the "real world" distance is between the two places.

Maps use *symbols* to represent real objects. Information on a map may be represented by lines, shapes, or colors. Some map symbols resemble or suggest the objects they represent. Two crossed pickaxes represent a mine or quarry on most maps. A long black line with small crossed lines represents railroad tracks. Large blue areas often represent bodies of water such as lakes, seas, and oceans. Green areas can represent forests. However, other map symbols may not look at all similar to the things they represent in real life. Cities are often represented as circles or large areas of color. A dot may represent a mountain peak on one map and 1,000 people on another. It is important to read the map's *legend,* or key, in order to understand how specific symbols are used on that map.

Most maps have legends to help identify and locate information. A legend shows which symbols are used on a map and what the symbols represent. The legend is usually printed in a box in the margin of the map. However, the legend can be located anywhere on the map.

A map sample with a grid

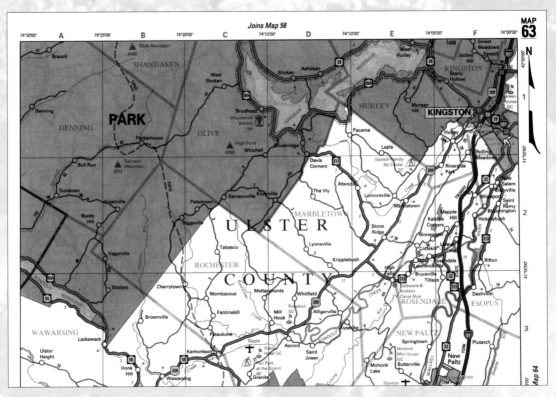

Most maps are drawn so that north is at the top of the page. An arrow on the map indicates which direction is north. To properly *orient,* or position, a map, make sure the arrow points north by using a compass.

Maps often have an *index* to help locate individual places. The index lists the locations in alphabetical order. Often each place in the index has a corresponding letter and number. For example, a street map is divided into an index grid of horizontal rows and vertical columns. The rows and columns are usually labeled with letters and numbers along the margins. Maple Street might be listed in the index followed by *G-3.* The letter and number, G-3, stand for Maple Street's location on the map's grid. Maple Street can be found where row G intersects with column 3 on the street map.

Map arrows indicating direction

TYPES OF MAPS

There are many types of maps. Each type has a special use. Some maps are used to measure distances and find places. Others are used to show rainfall, population, the locations of mineral deposits, or many other things. Maps can also show the boundaries of countries. They can show the locations of important geographical and geological features such as mountains, lakes, and rivers. They help us find our way from one place to another. Some maps have more than one purpose. Four of the most common categories of maps are *general reference, mobility, thematic,* and *inventory maps.*

A general reference map of Argentina

General reference maps are used to locate places. They often show such features as the boundaries of countries, mountain ranges, rivers, lakes, cities, and other significant landmarks. There are two important types of general reference maps. *Political maps* stress the boundaries between cities, states, and countries. *Physical maps* emphasize physical features such as mountains, rivers, lakes, and oceans.

3

Mobility maps are designed to help people move from one place to another. One of the most common mobility maps is a street map. This map shows the locations of streets, roads, and other features within cities. Highway maps and transit maps are also mobility maps. Airplanes navigate using mobility maps that show features viewed easily from the air. Ships use mobility maps that show water depths and land features that help with navigation.

A mobility map of Houston, Texas

Thematic maps show how features such as rainfall, population, or natural resources are spread over the Earth. A weather map on a TV news program is an example of a thematic map. This map may use colors or symbols to show how weather conditions are distributed over a specific area.

A thematic map of natural vegetation in Africa

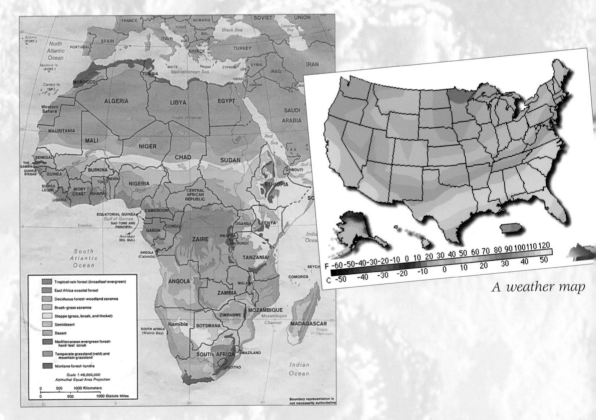

A weather map

4

Inventory maps show the exact locations of objects. A city map that shows each building is an inventory map. Maps of stadiums and concert halls that show the locations of all the seats are also inventory maps.

An inventory map of Yankee Stadium in New York

MAKING MAPS

The first step in creating a new map is to gather data. This is done through research, observation, and careful measurement of the selected area. *Cartographers,* or mapmakers, gather information from written accounts, previous maps, and other sources. They may interview local people to get information about significant features. In addition, scientists such as geologists may be consulted about the nature of the landforms in the area.

Next, observations and careful measurements are made of the area. Cartographers rely on *surveyors* to gather this information. Surveyors use special instruments to measure the locations of features and the relationships of those features to one another. They measure the distance from one object to another and the sizes of objects. They also measure the elevations of objects above (or below) sea level.

Surveyors use some simple instruments. These might include measuring tapes, compasses, and sighting rods. They also use complex electronic devices. These measure distances and angles with laser beams and radio waves. Modern surveyors use satellite photographs to gather detailed information about an area to map.

Finally surveyors record other information about the area to map. For example, a surveyor might record the exact location of a mountain peak and its elevation. Then he or she might note that the mountain has a sheer rock face on the northeast side and that the west side is forested. Other information such as the vegetation in the area, soil conditions, and local place names all add to the accuracy and usefulness of a map.

After all the information is gathered, the cartographer draws the map. He or she must consider the purpose of the map. This will help determine the map's scale and which symbols and colors are best suited to represent the map's features. Graphic artists often help cartographers design and draw maps. Today some maps are still drawn by hand, but many cartographers use computers to draw and color maps.

Global Positioning System (GPS)

A new piece of equipment is appearing in automobiles. It's also showing up on the bridges of ships and in hikers' and hunters' packs. It's called the GPS navigation system. *GPS* stands for "Global Positioning System." This system was put in place by the military in 1973. It is now used by cartographers to locate features to include on maps.

In an automobile, a GPS consists of a small screen with controls mounted to the dashboard. You can use it to automatically calculate your route. You can also find out where in the world you are if you're lost. The GPS tells you where you are anywhere on Earth within 100 meters (330 feet). The GPS is a system of 24 satellites positioned above the Earth and their ground-based tracking stations. The GPS in a car sends a signal to the satellites overhead. The signal includes the time it is sent. The GPS notes the time it takes for the signal to reach the satellite. Knowing this allows the system to calculate your distance from the satellite. The GPS determines your distance from at least three satellites. Then it uses a variation on the process of *triangulation* to calculate your location on the planet's surface. Your location on Earth is narrowed down to the place where the distances intersect.

A hand-held GPS

ANCIENT MAPS

People have drawn maps for thousands of years. One of the earliest maps was discovered in Iraq. The map was carved into a stone tablet. It showed the Earth as a disk surrounded by water with Babylon in its center. It was created about 4,500 years ago. The Babylonians were the first to divide a circle into 360 equal parts called *degrees*. This system is still used today to calculate *longitude* and *latitude*.

A Greek mathematician named Eratosthenes calculated the distance around the Earth in about 250 B.C.E. He and other Greek philosophers determined that the Earth was round, not flat. These developments contributed to the beginnings of cartography. A Greek astronomer and geographer named Ptolemy wrote an eight-volume *Geography* of the world in about the year 150. It contained maps of the known world and a list of more than 8,000 places with their locations.

Another early map is called the *Peutinger Table*. It is a copy of an earlier Roman map drawn by a monk from Alsace, France, in 1265. It was copied onto 12 sheets of parchment paper. The map is an

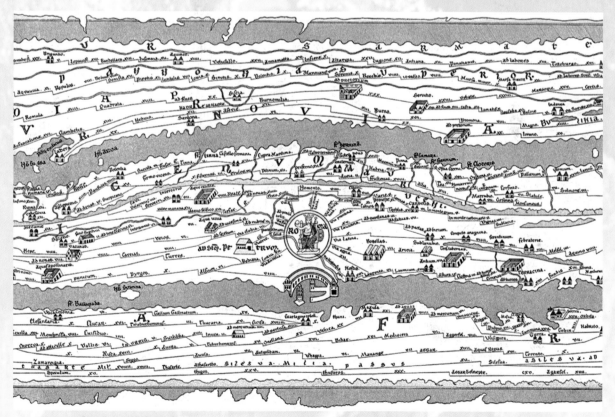

Central Italy and the adjacent countries from the Peutinger Table constructed about the year 393

elongated, or stretched-out, rectangle. Rome is distorted on the map. The distances from north to south are shortened and the distances from east to west are stretched out. Map experts still don't know how accurate the copy is.

Techniques for mapmaking also were invented in China during the Middle Ages. The oldest known Chinese map was drawn about 1137. Before Marco Polo arrived in 1271, most of China had been mapped, at least in a crude fashion. Jesuit missionaries who arrived in the 16th century prepared an atlas of Chinese maps.

Until the invention of the compass, early navigators coasted from one seaport to another. Many cartographers of this era did not make measurements of the areas they mapped. Instead they relied on information provided by explorers and other travelers. This information was often inaccurate. Sometimes it was completely wrong. Distances were often over- or underestimated. The relationships of map features to one another were greatly distorted. For example, a map from 1670 shows California as an island rather than part of the North American mainland. When a cartographer had no information about an area on a map, he sometimes used his imagination to fill in the missing parts. He might even include drawings of sea monsters and other creatures.

The magnetic compass was first used in 1187. One hundred years later, King Louis IX of France was presented with one of the first sea charts. It showed the whole Mediterranean Sea. The first sea charts were drawn on sheepskin and were called *portolans*. The biggest errors occurred because people assumed that a degree of latitude and a degree of longitude were equal.

It wasn't until the 17th century that this error was corrected. At this time, French astronomer Gian Domenico Cassini was head of the Paris Observatory. His work showed that as one gets closer to the poles, the distances between lines of longitude become shorter. He recorded books full of tables showing the exact hours, minutes, and seconds for eclipses of Jupiter's satellites. He used this data to help more accurately determine distances between Earth's *meridians,* or lines of longitude. Measurements based on his work showed the length of a meridian degree north of Paris to be shorter than one south of Paris. Then a new map of France was drawn with this information. King Louis XIV was surprised to find that the coast was actually 100 kilometers (60 miles) closer to Paris.

REAL PEOPLE IN THE GRAND CANYON

A majestic view of the Grand Canyon

The Grand Canyon is considered one of the most splendid natural wonders of the world. Nearly 5 million people travel to the Grand Canyon each year to view this spectacular example of erosion. The canyon stretches for 443 kilometers (277 miles) along the Colorado River in Arizona. It begins at Lee's Ferry, Arizona. It ends at Grand Wash Cliffs, just above Lake Mead.

The width and depth of the canyon vary from one place to another. Near Grand Canyon Village on the South Rim, its depth is about 1,515 meters (5,000 feet). From its high point on the North Rim, it is 1,820 meters (6,000 feet) down to the river. If you walk down to the river from the South Rim, the trail is 11.2 kilometers (7 miles) long. The hike from the North Rim along the North Kaibab Trail is 22.4 kilometers (14 miles). The width of the canyon at the village is 16 kilometers (10 miles). In other places it is as much as 29 kilometers (18 miles) wide.

The geologic history of the canyon is told in its layers of sedimentary rocks. These rocks include clues that help geologists figure out what was happening at the canyon since its beginning. That was over 1.7 billion years ago. The history of humans in the area is much shorter. However, it includes some fascinating tales of ancient people, brave explorers, and scientists who study the canyon today.

A survey map of the Grand Canyon, 1872–1873

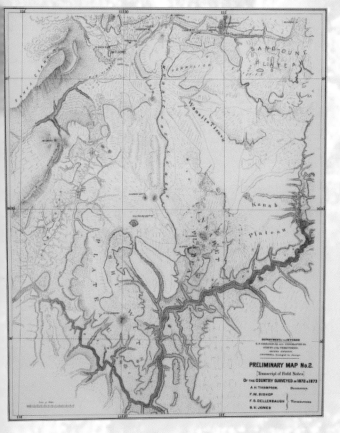

NATIVE AMERICANS IN THE CANYON

Split twig figures from the Grand Canyon

Native Americans have lived around the Grand Canyon for thousands of years. Evidence suggests they lived in the area over 10,000 years ago. The earliest known inhabitants were called the Desert Culture. They left behind small figures made from split twigs. The figures were of animals such as bighorn sheep and mule deer. These figures were preserved in caves formed in a layer of rock called the Redwall Limestone. The split twig figurines are the oldest record of humans living in the Grand Canyon. Some are 4,000 years old.

The Anasazi people lived in the canyon over 1,000 years ago. Before they moved into the canyon, they lived in the area around the canyon. They lived in *pithouses*, which were houses dug out of the ground. They hunted and gathered their food. They made baskets from the native yucca plant.

Around 1,200 years ago, the Anasazi started making pottery containers and growing crops. They began to move into the Grand Canyon at this time. They used caves in the canyon walls for homes. The caves protected them from harsh weather. Streams flowing into the canyon provided water. The Anasazi built irrigation ditches to channel the water. They built granaries to store grain. Spanish explorers, including Captain Garcia Lopez de Cardenas in 1540, called these Anasazi settlements *pueblos*. *Pueblo* is the Spanish word for "town."

The Anasazi mysteriously disappeared around 850 years ago. The Hopi people are believed to be the modern descendants of the Anasazi. They live in Arizona today.

Today about 650 Native Americans call the Grand Canyon home. They are members of the Havasupai tribe. *Havasupai* means "the people of the blue-green waters." Their village is called Supai. It is located in a remote region of the western Grand Canyon, near four waterfalls. The village has been occupied since about 1300. The Havasupai consider themselves the guardians of the Grand Canyon. Their culture is based on traditions that preserve and protect their surroundings.

JOHN WESLEY POWELL EXPLORES THE CANYON

Native Americans had lived in and around the Grand Canyon for thousands of years. But the canyon was a mystery to most Americans in the mid-19th century. Captain Garcia Lopez de Cardenas was probably the first European to see the canyon. He was sent north from Mexico in 1540 by Francisco Vasquez de Coronado. He was searching for the fabled Seven Cities of Gold. Cardenas and his party spent 3 days at the canyon, trying to get down to the river. They ran out of supplies and were forced to return to Mexico.

In 1869, Major John Wesley Powell (1834–1902) became the first person to explore the entire length of the canyon. Explorers had known about the canyon for over 300 years. However, no one had attempted the dangerous journey down this unknown length of the Colorado River.

John Wesley Powell

Powell was a natural explorer. As a young man, he traveled throughout Wisconsin, Illinois, Iowa, and Missouri. He explored the lengths of the Mississippi, Ohio, and Illinois Rivers, collecting specimens and studying their natural history. He taught himself about *zoology* (the study of animals), *botany* (the study of plants), and *geology* (the study of rocks and minerals).

This type of photograph is called a stereoview. When seen through a special "stereoscope," the two images merge into one, producing a three-dimensional effect. This stereoview shows Powell's boat in the Grand Canyon.

When he was 26 years old, Powell joined the Union army to fight in the Civil War (1861–1865). He was wounded, and his right arm was amputated below his elbow. This misfortune did not stop Major Powell. He returned to service in the army. When the Civil War ended, Powell began to explore the American West. He became fascinated with the Colorado and Utah Territories.

Powell made several trips to the Grand Canyon area to collect scientific information. Most of the United States had been mapped by this time, but the area that held the Grand Canyon was still a large blank on the map of the Southwest. Powell was determined to fill in the blank.

To gather more information, Powell decided to travel down the Green and Colorado Rivers with four rowboats and nine men. They started their trip on the Green River at the village of Green River, Wyoming. The expedition lasted 3 months. Powell's crew traveled through horrendous rapids and past high walls of sedimentary rock. Four crew members left the expedition along the way. One left before the rest of the party even reached the Grand Canyon. The other three tired of the dangers and left the party only days before they reached the end of the canyon. They left at the place that is now called Separation Canyon. Unfortunately these men were killed on their way north, being mistaken for criminals.

Near Foot of Toroweap, looking east at the Grand Canyon

Powell became a national hero. The expedition opened the way for further exploration of the Grand Canyon and the surrounding region. In 1873, Powell proposed a cooperative system of water management for the Southwest. He became the director of the U.S. Irrigation Survey in 1888. Powell's work as a geologist led to his appointment as the second director of the United States Geological Survey.

SCIENTISTS IN THE CANYON

Until 1963, humans had little impact on the Grand Canyon. Only a few people actually lived in or near the canyon. They made few changes to the landscape. The numbers of visitors to Grand Canyon National Park increased each year. This did have an impact on the environment, but for the most part, the visitors did not change the landscape.

In 1963, the gates of the Glen Canyon Dam closed. As a result, the Grand Canyon and the Colorado River were changed substantially. The dam was built to provide hydroelectric power to the western United States. The dam greatly reduced the volume of water flowing down the river and through the Grand Canyon. Further, the flow of water from the dam was regulated by the need for hydroelectric power, not by the requirements of the Colorado River animals and plants that called the area home. In addition to actually changing the shape of the Grand Canyon, the Glen Canyon Dam changed the ecosystem in the area.

Before 1963, annual floods washed tons of sediment down the river and through the Grand Canyon. The Colorado River was so full of sediment that early explorers said it was too thick to drink, but too thin to plow. Some of this sediment was deposited on beaches and sandbars. In the spring, runoff from snow caused the Colorado River to flood. Then sediment was washed and deposited higher up the canyon cliffs. Debris that clogged the river was washed away. The annual floods contributed to the form of the river. The dam stopped the flooding. Over time, beaches eroded and lost their sand. Debris built up in the river. The river landscape changed. So did habitats for the plants and animals that lived in the canyon.

A new group of people entered the Grand Canyon in response to these changes. Scientists called *hydrologists* came to study the flow of water and sediment. One of them, Dr. Julia Graf, was part of an important experiment in the canyon.

The U.S. Geological Survey decided to create a flood by allowing more water to flow through Glen Canyon Dam. They hoped the flood might restore some of the conditions that had existed before the dam was built. On March 26, 1996, the floodgates were opened. Twice the normal amount of water flowed through the canyon. Dr. Graf and other scientists observed the results. They hoped the increased water flow would erode and deposit enough sediment to restore the beaches and sandbars. Overall, the experiment was a success.

The artificial flood restored many beaches and sandbars. Backwaters were created where fish could spawn and increase in numbers. Vegetation survived the flood and provided shelter and food for animals in and around the river.

During the flood, Dr. Graf conducted a unique experiment of her own. She released 1,000 kilograms (2,200 pounds) of nontoxic red dye into the water. Then she measured how fast the dye flowed downstream and where it flowed. Using this data, she and other scientists were able to better predict the currents and flow of the Colorado River. This information will help scientists understand the forces that form the Grand Canyon. Then they will be able to develop new ways to preserve this great natural resource.

Dr. Graf releasing red dye into the river to gather data

The red Colorado River

QUESTIONS TO EXPLORE

- ■ Who were the earliest inhabitants of the Grand Canyon?
- ■ What is the oldest evidence of humans in the Grand Canyon?
- ■ Which Native American tribe inhabits the canyon now?

RIVERS AND CONTROLLING THE FLOW

A *river* is a large body of flowing water. Rivers have many *sources*. They often begin as small trickles of rainwater flowing downhill. The trickles join together to form rills, brooks, and streams. Most rivers begin in mountainous regions. Some rivers flow from lakes or glaciers. They flow toward lower elevations until they empty into another river, lake, ocean, or other large body of water.

RIVER FEATURES

The force of flowing water erodes earth materials such as sand, silt, clay, and even large boulders and carries the load downstream. A *channel* forms through which the river flows. The bottom of a river channel is called the *riverbed*. The edges of the channel are called the *banks*. As the river flows farther, the channel is eroded even more.

Rapids form where boulders obstruct the flow of water.

Many factors influence the shape of the land around river channels. Some of these include the underlying earth materials and the force of the water. The amount of sand and rock carried along by the river is also a factor. A river may carve a steep, V-shaped valley through a mountainous or hilly region. A fast-flowing river sometimes cuts a *gorge* or *canyon* into the landscape. Gorges and canyons are deep valleys with very steep sides.

Rapids may form where side canyons enter swift-flowing rivers. Large boulders, trees, and other debris are carried down to the main river. They obstruct the flow of water, creating rapids. The swirling currents of rapids can further erode the riverbank and carry more material downstream.

Waterfalls are formed when softer rock is worn away from the riverbed, leaving a step of harder rock. The river plunges over the step to form a waterfall. Waterfalls can be spectacular. Niagara Falls, on the border between the U.S. and Canada, drops 55 meters (180 feet). Yosemite Valley in California is known for its waterfalls that drop out of *hanging valleys,* hundreds of meters to the valley floors. Hanging valleys are smaller valleys that were left high above the main valley floor when a huge glacier carved out Yosemite.

Niagara Falls

As a river continues downstream, it often flows over wide areas of sediment called *flood plains.* This sediment is deposited by streams flowing into the main river. It is also deposited by the river itself when it overflows its banks and floods the nearby land. The flood plain is the area that a river overflows during floods. The flood plain of the Amazon River is hundreds of kilometers wide.

When rivers flow over flatter plains, they tend to wind back and forth across their channels. The loops that are formed in the channel are called *meanders.* Meanders are usually found where a river nears its mouth and the slope is gentle.

Large rivers may speed up as they near their mouths. They have collected water from many side streams along the way. The volume of water the river carries has increased. The force of this extra water causes the water to move faster.

The Mississippi flood plain, as seen by satellite

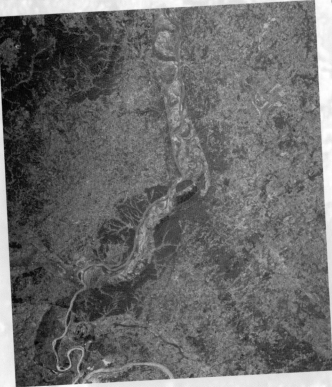

When the river actually reaches its mouth, it slows. The load of sediment it has carried is deposited. Larger particles are deposited first. Then the smaller silts and clays are deposited. This sediment forms small islands which create barriers against the water. The islands slow the water down even more. The river flows in channels around these small islands. The system of channels and islands that forms is known as a *delta.* Deltas often have triangular shapes when viewed from above.

Some rivers flow into the sea in a single broad channel called an *estuary*. The water in estuaries is a mix of fresh water from the river and salt water from the sea. As the tides and the river's currents change, the ratio of salt water to fresh water changes, too.

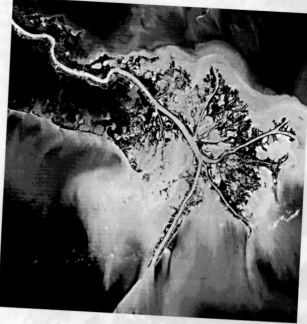

Rivers are not solitary streams flowing from the mountains to the sea. All major rivers are parts of systems. They include many *tributaries* that flow into the main river channel. The system of rivers, streams, and lakes that drain a region is called a *drainage net*. A drainage net consists of all of the rivers that flow through a region. The land covered by a drainage net is called a *drainage basin*. In the U.S., the Mississippi River drains the central portion of the country between the Appalachian Mountains and the Rocky Mountains. This large area of 2,990,000 square kilometers (1,150,000 square miles) covers 40 percent of the land area of the continental U.S. It includes thousands of rivers that eventually flow into the Mississippi River. This is the third-largest drainage basin in the world.

The Mississippi River delta, as photographed by satellite

The Continental Divide runs through the Rocky Mountains from Canada down into Mexico. At this imaginary line, rivers either flow east or west. If they flow east, they end up in the Mississippi River drainage basin. Flowing west, they become parts of other drainage basins. These basins include the one through which the Colorado River flows.

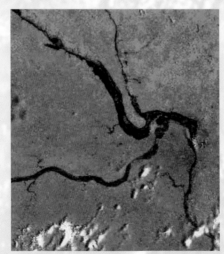
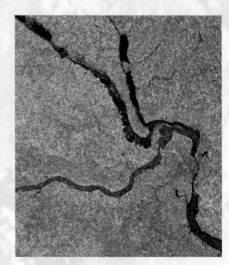

The flooding of the Mississippi River drainage basin

THE MISSISSIPPI RIVER

The source of the Mississippi River is a small lake in Minnesota called Lake Itasca. The river begins its 3,766-kilometer (2,340-mile) journey as a small, clear stream about 3.7 meters (12 feet) wide. The river flows north and then east through several lakes. Then it curves south, continuing its journey to the Gulf of Mexico.

The history of the Mississippi River begins more than 10,000 years ago. During the last ice age, glaciers deposited sediment and carved small lakes in the upper Mississippi River region. When the ice melted, the glacial runoff cut channels into the landscape. The runoff filled low spots eroded by the glacier, forming the many lakes of Minnesota. One of those lakes was Lake Itasca. From Lake Itasca, the Mississippi and its tributaries follow the channels eroded by the glaciers.

The Mississippi River is divided into two regions. It has a fast, clear-flowing section and a more sluggish, sediment-filled section. When it leaves Lake Itasca, the Mississippi is a clear river that flows through lakes and over waterfalls. Above St. Paul, Minnesota, the Mississippi is so narrow that larger boats cannot navigate it. From St. Paul south into Illinois, the river widens. There it is approximately 300 to 600 meters (1,000 to 2,000 feet) wide. However, it is still clear and flows fast.

The character of the Mississippi River changes just north of St. Louis, Missouri. There the Missouri River joins the Mississippi. The water of the Missouri is filled with sediment. The Mississippi takes on the familiar brown color of the Missouri. A few kilometers downstream, the Ohio River also joins the Mississippi. The volume of water doubles. The channel widens to 900 to 1,500 meters (3,000 to 5,000 feet). At this point, the lower Mississippi River begins and earns it name. *Mississippi* comes from two Algonquin words, *misi sipi,* that mean "big water."

As the river nears its mouth in the Gulf of Mexico, it slows and meanders through a flood plain that is 64 to 112 kilometers (40 to 70 miles) wide. For thousands of years, the river has deposited sediment along its course. The Mississippi River Valley is among the richest and most productive areas of farmland in the world. Finally the river flows past Baton Rouge, Louisiana, into a vast delta where it joins the Gulf of Mexico.

THE HUDSON RIVER

One of the most important rivers in the eastern United States is the Hudson River. The Hudson River extends 504 kilometers (315 miles). It runs from its source at Lake Tear of the Clouds in the Adirondack Mountains to New York Harbor. Its source is 1,315 meters (4,313 feet) above sea level. The upper portion of the river has many rapids and waterfalls. This region of New York State was once famous for textile and lumber mills powered by the Hudson River. The river drops into a valley carved by glaciers as it approaches Troy, New York. Here the riverbed is below sea level. As a result, tides from the faraway Atlantic Ocean affect the river's flow more than 240 kilometers (150 miles) away from its mouth.

An aerial view of the Hudson River flowing into the Atlantic Ocean

The river is more than 1.6 kilometers (1 mile) wide in places below Troy. As it nears its mouth, the channel cuts through cliffs known as the Palisades. These cliffs tower 90 to 170 meters (300 to 550 feet) above the riverbank. The drainage basin of the Hudson River covers about 34,760 square kilometers (about 13,370 square miles).

Henry Hudson first explored the Hudson River in 1609. Because of the wide, deep channel near the river's mouth and the presence of salt water, Hudson thought the river might be the fabled "Northwest Passage" from the Atlantic to the Pacific Ocean.

THE HISTORY OF FLOW CONTROL

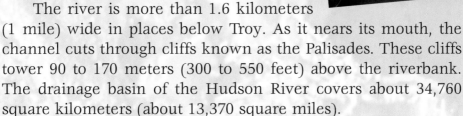

The Mississippi and Hudson Rivers share colorful histories. Since earliest exploration, both waterways have been important for commerce and transportation. Because of their significance, measures were taken on both rivers to control flooding and the flow of water.

Along the Mississippi, *levees* are an important means of controlling the flow of the river. A levee is an embankment or mound along a river's edge. Natural levees are formed when rivers deposit large quantities of sediment after a flood. Most artificial levees are much higher and wider than natural levees.

Along the Mississippi, levees range from 4.5 to 9 meters (15 to 30 feet) high. They are typically 2.4 meters (8 feet) wide at the top and 30 meters (100 feet) wide at the base. Levees are designed to hold back the river's flow from the surrounding land. When the river water rises, the levees prevent it from spilling onto the flood plain.

The first Mississippi levee was built on the river in 1718. Today 3,500 kilometers (2,200 miles) of levees line the Mississippi River. However, even the highest levees may be no match for extensive rains. The Mississippi Valley has flooded on several occasions in spite of the levees. In 1993, almost 2 months of rains in the region resulted in flooding along the upper Mississippi River system. Seventy-five thousand people were driven from their homes. Flooding caused more than $15 billion in damage. Many levees broke or were overwhelmed by the rising water.

Engineers and scientists continue to develop new ways to predict where floods will occur along the Mississippi. Monitoring stations, satellite photos, and radar images help predict rainfall and increased river flow. Excess water can be diverted into smaller channels to prevent the river from overflowing. Better building techniques make levees stronger. Dams along tributaries such as the Ohio and Missouri Rivers help control the rivers' volume. However, all of these efforts cannot stop the flow of water.

Some scientists and engineers object to the construction of levees that allow water to build up above the river's natural level. They say this causes worse flooding when the levees give way. These scientists and engineers often favor controlling water near the river's *headwaters,* or source. They suggest designating large strips of land along the riverbank as *floodways.*

The history of flow control on the Hudson River is very different from the history of the Mississippi. The Hudson provides a natural deep-water channel from its mouth at New York Harbor all the way to Albany. Ships can easily navigate its wide channel. Explorer Henry Hudson had hoped that the river would provide a passage to the Pacific. However, the Hudson River did not even reach as far as the Great Lakes.

In the late 1700s and early 1800s, it was very difficult to transport goods across the country. A connection was needed among the great oceans and rivers of the East to the lakes and rivers of the West. At that time, most goods traveled by water. Roads were primitive, and there were few railroads. A group of

New York citizens developed a plan to extend the Hudson River all the way to Buffalo, New York, on the shore of Lake Erie. The extension was to be a canal 8.5 meters (28 feet) wide and 1.2 meters (4 feet) deep.

At first, the proposal seemed impossible and too expensive. But after much planning, construction of the Erie Canal began on July 4, 1817. Eight years later, the first canal boat made the journey from Buffalo to New York City. The canal was 581 kilometers (363 miles) long. Eighty-two *locks* lifted the boats from sea level on the Hudson to 210 meters (689 feet) above sea level at Buffalo. The locks were like stairs made of water. Each lock closed off a section of the canal. Then that section was flooded to raise the water level.

The waters of the Great Lakes were joined with the Hudson River. Barges carrying people and goods traveled along the river. The trip between New York City and Buffalo took about 3.5 days. The canal was a great success. Goods traveled east and west more efficiently than ever before. The Erie Canal is still used today. However, most of the commercial traffic that once traveled the canal now moves by railroad or highway.

QUESTIONS TO EXPLORE

- **What factors influence the shape of the land around river channels?**
- **Where is the Mississippi drainage basin?**
- **What is a drainage net?**

SHAPES OF THE EARTH

EARTHQUAKES, VOLCANOES, AND MOUNTAINS

Most of the time, people can't feel it, but the surface of the Earth is constantly in motion. To understand how the Earth's surface moves, it is important to understand how the Earth is constructed. The Earth is made of layers. The outer layer is called the *crust*. The crust is broken into 30 pieces called *tectonic plates*. These pieces fit together like a puzzle. The plates are about 100 kilometers (60 miles) thick in most places. However, they may be as little as 8 kilometers (5 miles) thick or as great as 200 kilometers (120 miles) thick. The plates cover the entire planet and form the surface of the continents and ocean floors.

Beneath the crust is another layer called the *mantle*. The mantle is made of molten rock, or *magma*. The magma can reach temperatures between 1,300°C and 2,000°C (2,400°F and 3,600°F). The crust floats on this molten rock. As the pieces of crust float, they are pushed around by currents in the magma. On average, this movement is usually only about 10 centimeters (4 inches) per year. Although it is very slight, the movement of the Earth's plates has dramatic results.

The tectonic plates have been moving for hundreds of millions of years. As they move, the plates push against each other. When two plates push directly against each other, the force causes them to buckle and crumble. The plates push upward and create great folds in the Earth's surface. This is called *uplift*. The great mountain ranges of the Earth were all formed by uplift. In Asia, the Himalayas were formed when two plates collided about 40 million years ago. They formed the world's highest mountain range. The Appalachian and Rocky Mountains in the U.S. were formed this way, too. The formation of mountains through uplift takes millions of years. The Himalayas are still growing. But their growth is so slow that it takes sophisticated scientific instruments to measure it.

An aerial view of the Himalayas, with Mount Everest, the tallest peak on Earth, in the center of the photograph

Mountains are also built when the magma from the mantle pushes up a portion of the crust. This forms a bulge in the Earth's surface. These mountains are called *dome mountains*. They are usually rounded and not as high as uplifted mountains. The Black Hills in South Dakota are an example of dome mountains.

The place where two plates move past each other is often an area of *faults,* or breaks in the Earth's surface. The ground can shift drastically as the plates slide past each other. This can cause powerful earthquakes. Sometimes the plates get stuck at places along a fault and cannot move. When this happens, energy builds up. Eventually the plates break free. Then they may quickly shift several meters, causing an earthquake. The San Andreas fault is a long fault traveling from north to south for hundreds of kilometers in California. Movements of the plates that form this fault caused destructive earthquakes in the San Francisco Bay Area in 1906 and 1989 and in Los Angeles in 1994. Over millions of years, the shape of California will continue to change dramatically as one plate moves north and the other moves south.

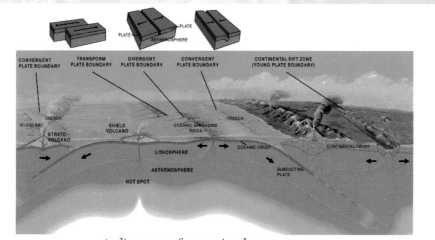

A diagram of tectonic plate movement

Earthquakes are also caused by volcanic activity. Volcanic earthquakes are generally less powerful than tectonic earthquakes. However, they signal the presence of another powerful force, volcanoes. Volcanoes are formed in several general areas. These are areas where plates collide and areas where plates pull apart, or *rift*. Volcanoes also form over *hot spots* in the middle of plates.

The Cascade Range includes volcanoes found in northern California, Oregon, and Washington State. The Cascades are an example of what happens when one plate is *subducted,* or shoved under another plate. Cracks in the overriding plate allow magma from below to erupt. This forms *stratovolcanoes*. Many stratovolcanoes are located in the Ring of Fire, a zone of volcanoes surrounding the Pacific Ocean. This band of volcanic activity is where the Pacific Plate collides with the continental plates of North America and Asia. Mount St. Helens is part of the Ring of Fire. It is a volcano in the Cascades in Washington State. Its eruption in 1980 caused widespread destruction.

The Hawaiian volcanoes which form the Hawaiian Islands are examples of volcanoes formed over a hot spot. The Pacific Plate on which the volcanoes are formed travels over a hot spot in the mantle. As it moves, new volcanoes form over the hot spot. The Hawaiian Islands form a chain of islands. Kauai is the oldest island and is composed of extinct volcanoes. The island of Hawaii is the youngest Hawaiian Island. Kilauea, on the island of Hawaii, is still erupting. Just offshore from the island of Hawaii, a new volcano called Loihi is building up from the ocean floor as it moves over the hot spot. Maybe hundreds of years from now, it will create the newest Hawaiian Island.

A lava fountain 450 meters (1,485 feet) high bursts from Pu`u`O`o in Hawaii in September 1984.

The tallest mountain in the world is a volcano. Mauna Kea is a volcano that makes up part of the island of Hawaii. It is an example of a *shield volcano*, made from many thin layers of lava. The Hawaiian Islands are the peaks of volcanic mountains that jut above the surface of the ocean. Mauna Kea reaches 5,965 meters (19,680 feet) from the ocean floor to the surface. Then it continues to rise another 4,181 meters (13,796 feet) above sea level. From its base to its summit, Mauna Kea is 10,146 meters (33,476 feet) high. That makes it taller than Mount Everest. However, more than half of Mauna Kea's height is below the surface of the ocean.

A diagram of Mauna Kea above and below the water

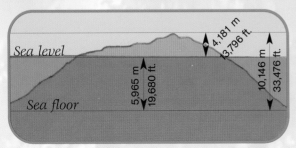

Sea level

4,181 m
13,796 ft.

10,146 m
33,476 ft.

5,965 m
19,680 ft.

Sea floor

Other volcanoes form in *rift zones*. These are places where two plates are pulling apart. There are rifts in Africa and under the Atlantic Ocean. The biggest rift in the Atlantic Ocean is called the Mid-Atlantic Ridge. Iceland is located at the northern end of the ridge. From 1963 to 1967, volcanic eruptions along the ridge created a whole new island off the coast of Iceland. This was the island of Surtsey. In 1973, a volcano on the island of Heimaey, Iceland, erupted, forcing many of its residents to leave. People returned and rebuilt their homes after the eruption ended.

WAVE ACTION

Waves pound against the coast and constantly change its shape. Soft or sandy soils may be washed onto the coastline and deposited there. The sand and soil form *beaches* and *sand dunes*. Sand, silt, and gravel build up on ridges parallel to the shore along some coastlines. These small islands are separated from the coast by short stretches of water. The sandy ridges are called *barrier islands*. The Atlantic and Gulf Coasts of the U.S. are lined with barrier islands. These include Hatteras Island, North Carolina, and Padre Island, Texas.

Some barrier islands were formed when glaciers deposited *moraines* along the coast. Moraines are hills formed by rocks and soils pushed along by glaciers. Over time, these small islands became covered with sand and silt. Long Island, New York, and Nantucket Island, Massachusetts, are examples of barrier islands formed by glacial moraines.

Waves pound the shoreline.

Waves also erode the shoreline. The force of waves pounding the coast forces air into the cracks of rocks. The air weakens the rocks over time. The crashing waves also contain materials such as sand and gravel that erode the base of sea cliffs. The overhanging cliffs eventually crumble into the ocean. Soft soils along coastlines are worn away to form *bays*. Harder rocks remain to form *headlands*. Follow any coastline of the United States on a map. You will see that such features formed by wave action against the shore are clearly visible.

GLACIERS

Glaciers are large, moving expanses of ice. They form when the rate of snowfall is greater than the melting rate. Over time, a large sheet of snow accumulates. The snow at the bottom of the mass is compressed into a sheet of ice. The glacial ice starts to flow slowly because of its great weight. Because the ice is so heavy, pressure at the bottom causes the lower portions to melt. The ice begins to slip further.

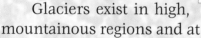
Glaciers are very unpredictable and ever-changing.

Glaciers exist in high, mountainous regions and at cold latitudes near the North and South Poles. During long periods of cold temperatures on Earth, called *ice ages*, glaciers covered much of the Northern Hemisphere. The last ice age began about 250,000 years ago. The ice sheets and glaciers did not recede from North America and Europe until about 10,000 years ago.

Glaciers usually move quite slowly down mountainsides. In general, glaciers travel only about 100 meters (about 300 feet) per year. However, glaciers in Iceland and Alaska have been recorded at speeds of more than 100 meters per day.

Glaciers change and shape the land in several ways. As the ice moves across the land, it picks up loose boulders, sand, and other materials. These become frozen within the glacier. The rocks frozen in the bottom of the glacier scour and polish the rock over which the heavy mass of ice moves. The valley through which a glacier moves is widened and its floor is flattened. A typical glacial valley is U-shaped in cross section.

Yosemite Valley is a good example of a glacial valley. The *fjords* of Alaska are examples of glacial valleys that were formed when glaciers cut deep valleys in the coast. The valleys were then filled by the sea.

Often glaciers may pick up loose boulders and carry them kilometers away from their original positions. When the ice melts, the boulders are left in new places. The boulders are called *erratics* because they often look quite different from the other rocks in the area.

Glaciers also push or bulldoze loose earth materials, forming moraines along the front and sides of the glacier. They are made of a mixture of boulders, pebbles, and clay. Moraines may form hills high

Yosemite Valley in California

enough to make good ski runs. In other places, if a glacier melted fairly quickly, the glacial debris forms a *till plain* or a blanket of *till* over the land. Till is any unsorted earth material that is directly deposited by glacial ice.

Glaciers retreat when the weather warms above freezing. Then ice melts faster than snow piles up. Meltwater from retreating glaciers also creates and changes landforms. Meltwater deposits are usually well sorted and are made of particles that are mostly the same size. Meltwater can form rivers which carry sediments from the glacier. Some sediments may have been ground to fine, light-colored silt and clay. The silt and clay color the meltwater white. This white-colored meltwater is known as *glacial milk*. Eventually the silt and clay are deposited by the meltwater in lake bottoms or other basins.

Outwash plains are flat areas of sand and gravel. People often mine the sand and gravel in these areas, leaving behind what is known as a "gravel pit." *Eskers* are snaking ridges of sand and gravel. They are formed from deposits left by meltwater rivers meandering beneath the glacial ice. *Kames* are steep-sided hills of sand and gravel. Kames are formed when meltwater flowing across the surface of a glacier deposits sediments in the glacier's crevasses.

CAVES AND SINKHOLES

Landforms can also be found under the Earth's surface. Caves and sinkholes are examples of landforms that are sometimes hidden below ground. There are several kinds of caves, and they vary in size. They may be small depressions in hillsides or networks of caverns extending underground for kilometers.

Large caverns may form in limestone where there is a lot of rain. Streams and rainwater absorb carbon dioxide from the air and soil. The water turns into a weak form of *carbonic acid.* Over thousands of years, the acid dissolves the limestone and creates caverns underground. The caverns are often filled with spectacular mineral deposits. Deposits that hang from the ceiling like icicles are called *stalactites.* Those that grow up from the cave floor are called *stalagmites.* Carlsbad Caverns National Park in New Mexico is a network of limestone caves famous for the beauty of its underground chambers.

Carlsbad Caverns in New Mexico

The depth of a limestone cave is determined by the height of the *water table.* The water table is the level of the groundwater in an area. *Groundwater* is the water that has seeped into the ground. As the water table rises, caverns are created closer to the surface. As the water table lowers, caves develop farther underground.

When a cavern forms too close to the surface, the ceiling may collapse, forming a *sinkhole.* Sometimes sinkholes are described as "bottomless pits." This isn't true. They do have bottoms, although the holes may be very deep. Sometimes sinkholes form beneath highways or buildings. Then the structures may fall into the sinkholes. Sinkholes in Florida have swallowed houses and automobiles.

Some caves are formed by the action of waves against sea cliffs. These caves are called *sea caves.* If part of the rock in a sea cave collapses, a *sea arch* may form.

Sand carried by strong winds can carve caves in the sides of rocks and hills. This type of cave is common in the American

Southwest. Another type of cave forms in volcanic areas. A *lava tube* is a cave that forms in cooling lava. A tube forms when some lava cools more quickly than the rest. The remaining lava drains out of the tunnel the cooled lava has formed. Thurston Lava Tube on the island of Hawaii is an example of a lava tube in an active volcano area. Lava tubes are also located in regions where volcanoes no longer erupt. One such place is Mushpot Cave in Lava Beds National Monument in northern California. Another is Surprise Caves and Indian Tunnel in Craters of the Moon National Monument in Idaho.

Thurston Lava Tube in Hawaii

THE STORY OF MOUNT SHASTA

The following is adapted from an account of a night in a snowstorm on Mount Shasta. The story is based on an article by John Muir. The article was published in the September 1877 issue of Harper's New Monthly Magazine. Muir (1838–1914) was a naturalist and explorer. He traveled extensively throughout California and wrote about his adventures.

The climb to the top of Mount Shasta is usually undertaken in summer, during favorable weather. Then the deep snows have melted from the lower slopes. At that time, storms are much less likely to occur. But whatever the season, Shasta's peak is covered in a constant layer of snow and ice. I agreed to attempt the climb in spring in order to take barometric observations from the summit.

My companion, Jerome Fay, and I began our climb on April 30, 1875. We took packhorses to carry supplies. We made our way toward a camp about 16 kilometers (10 miles) up the mountain trail. We planned to camp overnight and then get an early start the next morning.

We had not expected to encounter snow 1.5 meters (5 feet) deep on the trail. We pushed on throughout the day, but made slow progress. As the Sun began to set, we realized we would not make our destination by nightfall. Determined to go on, we left the horses. We carried a day's provisions and our blankets up the slope to the timberline. There we set up camp, sheltered by a block of red lava. We slept only 2 hours. At two A.M., we arose to a fine, starry sky. After cooking our breakfast of venison on the coals, we set off for the summit.

Our pulses raced as we were surrounded by the beauty of the morning. We plunged ahead, hardly stopping for breath. Our boots clomped over the red lava apron that leads up the west side of the mountain. We made our way toward the smaller of the two cone-shaped summits. We crossed the gorge that separates the two peaks and swung around the Whitney Glacier. The hot *fumaroles*, vents through which volcanic gases and steam escape, hissed and belched as we hiked upward. By 7:30 A.M., we were at the summit.

Fay and I marveled at the landscapes that surrounded us. I took the required barometric measurements and looked to my companion. At first, I did not understand his frown as he stared southward. As I looked into the Shasta Valley, I knew why he was dismayed. The valley was filled with gray and purple cumulus clouds. My first thought was how beautiful the storm clouds were on the mountain. Then I realized our danger.

Fay and I immediately began our descent. We moved slowly down the mountain. By one P.M. the storm reached the summit and began pounding us with hailstones. As we stood beside a hissing fumarole, I observed that the hailstones were of an unusual shape, with six straight sides and a domelike crown. Fay was interested less in the shape of the hailstones and more in the condition of the storm. All at once, the violence of the storm hit us with its might.

Had I been alone, I might have attempted the descent. However, Fay convinced me that the only sane course was to ride out the storm near the hissing hot springs. The temperature quickly dropped more than 11°C (20°F). The wind became violent. Lightning flashed. We had only one chance. We removed as much clothing as possible and lay in the fuming mud on the edge of the hot springs. Thus we spent the night, freezing on one side and boiling on the other.

As we lay in this state, both threatened and protected by the mountain, my mind wandered to the origins of Shasta. The giant cone of Mount Shasta stands in constant snow. It can be seen from anywhere within a 80- to 160-kilometer (50- to 100-mile) radius around the mountain. This majestic mountain of volcanic ashes and lava rises 4,317 meters (14,162 feet) above sea level. It towers more than 3,000 meters (almost 10,000 feet) above the plain on which it sits. Shasta originated from repeated eruptions that built it upward and outward like the trunk of a tree. The mountain is more than 250,000 years old. Its two peaks are the results of multiple eruptions.

The remains of Shasta's violent history can still be found on the sides of the mountain. Gases, mud, steam, and boiling water spew up through cracks from the *magma,* or molten rock, below. The fumarole in which we were lying was one such outlet.

As quickly as it came upon us, the storm ended. The sky became clear and filled with stars. The temperature was still too cold to attempt our descent of the mountain, so we remained in our cooker until morning. Then we trudged down the mountain in our frozen, stiff clothes. Luckily we were met at our camp by a friend with horses. As we descended, we could feel the Sun's warmth on our backs. I looked over my shoulder at the great white cone of Mount Shasta. The ordeal of the previous night seemed like a faraway dream.

A Cascades Volcano

Mount Shasta is located 65 kilometers (40 miles) south of the California-Oregon border. At 4,317 meters (14,162 feet), it is the second-highest mountain in the Cascade Range. Mount Shasta is an example of a *stratovolcano.* Stratovolcanoes are volcanoes composed of lava flows, ash, and other material blown out by explosive activity. Shastina, the prominent cone on the west flank of Shasta, was active about 9,200 years ago. The Hotlum cone at Shasta's peak was active only a few centuries ago.

TOPOGRAPHIC MAPS

A map is a picture of the Earth's surface. Although most maps are drawn on flat paper, the Earth has many bumps and curves. These changes in elevation are difficult to show on a flat surface. *A topographic map* is a special type of map that shows changes in elevation. At first, a topographic map may look like a lot of squiggles and blotches of color. However, the map can provide a great deal of information. First you must understand how the lines and symbols are used.

The most obvious feature of a topographic map is the system of curved lines that covers the map. These lines are called *contours,* and they are usually brown. Each contour represents a specific elevation. Elevations on U.S. maps published by the U.S. Geological Survey (USGS) are measured in feet above sea level. In countries where the metric system is used, elevations are measured in meters. Surveyors measure elevations when they gather the information to create a new map.

When you move your finger along a contour line on a topographic map, the elevation is the same at every point on the line. Your path would be flat if you walked along the course the contour represents in the real world. You would not go up- or downhill. Contours are always connected at both ends. If you follow a contour line on a topographic map, you will always return to the place where you began. Sometimes the ends of a contour run off the map page. But eventually they connect if you enlarge the map or follow them onto an adjacent map.

A hill on a topographic map is represented by rings of contour lines. The rings become smaller and smaller as they approach the top of the hill. If you move from one contour to

Colors Used on Most USGS Topographic Maps

Green Major vegetation: forest, brush, and orchards

Blue Water: lakes, streams, rivers, springs, marshes, oceans, and glaciers

Red Highways or boundaries

Black Human-made structures and place names

White Absence of vegetation: prairies, meadows, tundra, and deserts

Brown Land features, lava flows, sand areas, and contour lines

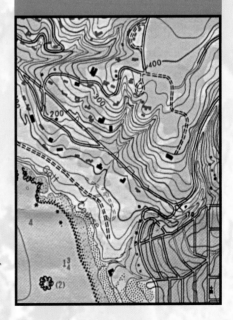

A topographic map of Yosemite Valley

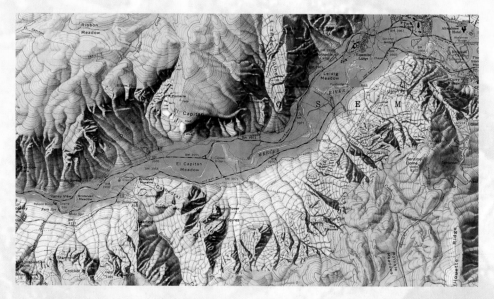

another, you move either up or down in elevation. In real life, if you walk across contour lines represented on the map, you will go either uphill or downhill.

Elevation changes rapidly if contours are close together. A steep hill is represented by closely spaced contours. If the contours are farther apart, they represent a more gradual slope. Some contour lines are thicker than others and have elevations printed on them. These are called *index contours*. The numbers tell the elevations of the index contours. Index contours help determine whether the elevation is rising or falling.

The United States Geological Survey (USGS)

Topographic maps are made by the United States Geological Survey (USGS). This federal agency was established in 1879. Its task is to map, study, and interpret the geology, hydrology, and topography of the country. USGS surveyors use the latest scientific instruments to create accurate maps. They have created topographic maps of the entire country. In addition, the USGS investigates natural hazards such as volcanoes, earthquakes, and landslides.

Topographic maps contain other important information. A scale is printed on the bottom of the map in the margin. In the U.S., the standard scale of many topographic maps is 1:24,000 (1 inch equals 24,000 inches or 2,000 feet). The scale is shown as a ratio, graphic scale, or both. In other countries, the scale is given in meters. The text in the margin also states the *contour interval*. This is the change in elevation between any two contour lines. A contour interval of 3 meters (10 feet) means that the elevation of each contour line is 3 meters (10 feet) higher or lower than the one next to it.

Topographic maps contain much more information than changes in elevation. Symbols and colors represent natural landforms and structures made by people. USGS topographic maps use a standard set of colors and symbols to represent objects.

AERIAL PHOTOGRAPHY

Two high-altitude photos show Washington, D.C. To the left is a photo taken with normal film. To the right is an infrared photo.

A map is a "bird's-eye" view of an area of the Earth. In the past, this view was only available in a *cartographer's,* or mapmaker's, imagination. The mapmaker observed and measured the land's features. Then these features were translated into a picture with an overhead viewpoint. For hundreds of years, this overhead, or "bird's-eye" view depended upon the skill and imagination of the cartographer.

Today nothing is left to the imagination. One of the most powerful tools cartographers use now is *aerial photography.* Photographs taken from airplanes or satellites are used to show how the Earth appears from above. Aerial photographers use sophisticated cameras and other sensing instruments. These allow them to take detailed pictures of the Earth. The photographs can be overlapped to show large areas. The views shown in the photos help cartographers draw more accurate maps.

Aerial photographs are taken from many heights. Those taken by airplanes flying at altitudes of 1,500 to 18,000 meters (about 5,000 to 60,000 feet) show more detail. However, it is necessary to take more photographs to cover an area. Satellites fly much higher, usually at altitudes greater than 240 kilometers (150 miles). In general, higher altitudes show larger areas but less detail. Lower altitudes show smaller areas but more detail. Both types of photographs are helpful to cartographers. The USGS has used aerial photographs to create maps and collect other data since 1950.

Scientists use special instruments to measure aerial photographs. The science of *photogrammetry* involves making these measurements and interpreting information in aerial photographs. The photographs are sometimes distorted and must be corrected before they are used to create maps. For example, hills often appear larger than valleys within the same area. This distortion occurs because the hills are closer to the camera than the valleys. *Photogrammetrists* correct photographs for this type of distortion. They also identify objects in aerial photographs and measure the distances from one object to another.

Some aerial photographs are taken with sensors other than cameras. Such sensors detect electromagnetic energy invisible to the unaided human eye. *Infrared photographs* can penetrate clouds and haze in the atmosphere. Infrared photos can also show diseased vegetation, and they are useful in showing bodies of water. Landsat satellites orbit the Earth and use *multispectral scanners* to capture images of the planet. These images are used to improve the accuracy of maps and to create special-purpose maps.

The Himalayas

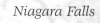

Niagara Falls

NATIONAL PARKS

The stars represent five of the hundreds of U.S. parks.

There are more than 350 national parklands in the United States. The National Park System includes 20 different types of areas that are protected and preserved for use by U.S. citizens. These include parks, monuments, historic sites, memorials, seashores, and battlefields. Every state except Delaware has at least one national parkland. The parklands in the National Park System are visited by about 275 million people each year.

The U.S. was the first country to establish a national park. Fur trappers and explorers told tales of a magnificent country called Yellowstone. In 1870, an expedition led by General Henry D. Washburn explored and surveyed the Yellowstone region. Yellowstone is located in the states of Wyoming, Montana, and Idaho. Washburn returned home convinced that this territory should be preserved for future generations. In 1872, Congress established Yellowstone National Park as the world's first national park. Four more parks were established in the 1890s. They were Yosemite, Sequoia, and General Grant (now Kings Canyon) in California and Mount Rainier in Washington.

Over the years, a steady stream of parks and other parklands joined the National Park System. National parks vary greatly in size. Some parklands are simply individual historic homes or monuments. Some parklands are quite large, such as Wrangell–St. Elias National Park in Alaska. This park is larger than the state of Hawaii.

Parklands are preserved for three important reasons. Some parklands contain unusual natural features. The Grand Canyon in Arizona, the Everglades in Florida, and Cape Cod National Seashore in Massachusetts are examples of parks with unique characteristics. Parklands are also preserved for their historic value. The Native American ruins at Ocmulgee National Monument in Georgia and the White House are two examples of parklands with historic value. The third group of parklands is preserved for its recreational value. Lake Mead in Nevada provides boating, fishing, and other aquatic sports. Wolf Trap Farm Park for the Performing Arts in Virginia is a popular center for music, dance, and theater.

National parks preserve the impressive beauty of the landforms that are a part of the United States. These landforms can be experienced firsthand by visiting many of the national parks located throughout the country. A quick tour of a few of these parks shows how they have been preserved.

BIG BEND NATIONAL PARK, TEXAS

Big Bend National Park is one of the last wilderness areas in Texas. The park covers more than 320,000 hectares (800,000 acres). Its name comes from the long, sweeping curves made by the Rio Grande River as it flows through the park. The amazing shapes of the rock outcrops found at Big Bend amazed early visitors

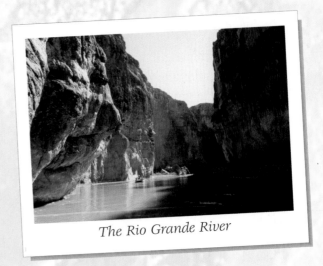

The Rio Grande River

and explorers. The geologic formations have been described as "staggering" by almost everyone who views them.

The history of Big Bend's landforms is evident everywhere within the park. The effects of the Rio Grande River on this desert landscape can be seen along its banks. Evidence of uplift is present in the mountains and faults that are found in the park.

The Chisos Mountain Range lies completely within the park. Much of the rock of these mountains was formed from magma cooling beneath the Earth's surface. Erosion has made it visible today.

Three deep canyons reveal over 500 million years of geological history in Big Bend National Park. Sediments deposited 300 million years ago by a prehistoric sea became the layers of rock visible in the canyons today. Sand dunes cover parts of Boquillas Canyon. Calcite cliffs show how acid mixed with rainwater can etch limestone.

EVERGLADES NATIONAL PARK, FLORIDA

The Everglades

Everglades National Park is the largest subtropical wilderness in the United States. The park is home to various animal and plant species. The dominant feature of the park is its abundance of water. However, human intervention has altered the natural flow of water through the park.

The park's water comes primarily from the slow-moving Kissimmee River in central Florida. The river's natural flow moves south through the Everglades to the Gulf of Mexico. However, for more than 100 years, dikes, canals, levees, and floodgates have changed that flow. The result is that less and less water is able to enter the Everglades environment. In addition, the groundwater and runoff have become polluted with harmful chemicals such as nitrates and pesticides. The Everglades ecosystem has been severely disturbed by the altered flow of water through the system.

The Everglades are known for several interesting land features. These include *freshwater sloughs, marl prairies, woody hammocks,* and *sinkholes.* Sloughs are wet, marshy areas that often include a slow-moving channel or backwater. Marl prairies lie over a loose mixture of clay and shell fragments. Hammocks, or hummocks, are low hills often covered with trees rising above a plain or swampy area. Sinkholes are areas that have collapsed over underground caverns.

The animals and plants that live in the Everglades include Florida panthers, alligators, manatees, green anole lizards, sawgrass, and mangrove trees. Several species, including the Florida panther, are endangered.

GLACIER BAY NATIONAL PARK, ALASKA

The forces of nature are vividly apparent in Glacier Bay National Park. Two hundred years ago, Glacier Bay was a small indentation in the coast of Alaska. Since that time, glaciers have advanced and then retreated to reveal massive fjords. The fjords were carved by glaciers over millions of years. The glaciers at Glacier Bay today are remnants of the Little Ice Age that occurred only 4,000 years ago. They tower 60 meters (200 feet) above the icy water of the bay. Large chunks of the glaciers often break off to form icebergs.

Glacier Bay National Park

The peak of Mount Fairweather lies within the boundaries of the park, only a few kilometers from the bay. Mount Fairweather towers 4,663 meters (15,300 feet) above sea level. The glaciers get their start in the Fairweather Mountain Range. They move slowly down to the bay.

MAMMOTH CAVE NATIONAL PARK, KENTUCKY

Mammoth Cave National Park is the largest known cave system in the world. It includes about 320 kilometers (200 miles) of explored passages. The caves in the system are known for their beauty, as well as their size. They feature many unusual cave formations such as gypsum flowers, cave needles, stalactites, stalagmites, and crystals of many shapes and sizes.

Mammoth Cave National Park

Mammoth Cave represents two different cave forming processes. The Green River carved many of the caves' horizontal passages. Other chambers were created when groundwater seeped into the limestone cave walls. The water absorbed carbon dioxide from the air and soil and formed weak carbonic acid. The acid dissolved the limestone. The result was the many chambers of Mammoth Cave.

Today the lowest level of the caves contains Echo River, a subterranean stream. Its channel is about 110 meters (360 feet) below the surface. Several waterfalls are also found within the cave walls.

VOYAGEURS NATIONAL PARK, MINNESOTA

Voyageurs National Park is named for the French fur traders who first explored the area in the 18th and 19th centuries. The park is dominated by water. Over one-third of the park is covered by lakes, rivers, and streams. This vast expanse of waterways is called the Voyageurs Highway. Upon entering the park, visitors leave their cars in a parking lot. All travel is by water, the way the early explorers traveled here. The park presents visitors with a glimpse of life in the region when the first traders and settlers arrived.

The network of waterways is the result of at least four different glacial periods. The glaciers bulldozed their way through the land, gouging out the landscape to form many small depressions and valleys. When the glaciers retreated, the low areas filled with water to form lakes and rivers. The effects of erosion and deposition are found throughout the park. It is said that the Voyageurs Highway is a gift from the glaciers.

The bedrock of Voyageurs National Park is 2.7 billion years old. The park is at the southern end of a region called the Canadian Shield. The rocks that make up this area are among the oldest exposed rocks on Earth.

Voyageurs National Park

THE EYE OF THE NEEDLE

Before

After

Near Fort Benton, Montana, is an isolated spot along a rugged and scenic part of the Missouri River. A beautiful natural landmark was there. It was a delicate, gently curving, 3.3-meter (11-foot) high arch. It was made of sandstone. It had been worn into its shape by centuries of water and wind erosion. Travelers rafting along the river often paused to take photographs or simply enjoy the beauty of the arch. Explorers Meriwether Lewis and William Clark traveled the Missouri River in 1805 on their passage across the country. They camped near the arch and wrote about it in their journal. They called the landform the "Eye of the Needle."

The arch was located in a deep-river canyon region called White Cliffs. White Cliffs is part of a 60-hectare (149-acre) preserve along the Missouri River. It was not easy to travel to the arch. It was only reachable by raft, and then by foot up steep rock chutes from the river. Because of its location, the arch was only visible from downstream. A traveler had to look back from a bluff 38 meters (125 feet) above the water to see the Eye of the Needle.

During Memorial Day weekend in 1997, vandals destroyed the arch. They broke the delicate sandstone into crumbled pieces. If caught, the vandals each face up to 10 years in prison and $100,000 in fines. Some people feel the punishment is not great enough. When the damage was discovered, outraged citizens raised funds as reward money to help bring the criminals to justice. Other citizens wondered what to do about the arch. Three plans were suggested.

One plan proposed to rebuild the arch. Natural sandstone could be used. A more durable artificial material could also be used, like the one used to create rocks in zoos. The potential cost was the major objection to this plan. Rebuilding the arch in such a remote wilderness area with no easy access would be expensive. Some people felt that an artificial, rebuilt arch was not the same as a natural arch. They believed money should not be spent to rebuild natural wonders of the world.

On the other side of the debate, many people thought money could still be raised to rebuild the arch. People from all over the country mailed donations. Some people argued that natural objects are repaired all the time. A stalactite destroyed by a vandal in a Montana cave was reattached to the ceiling of the cave. No one objected to that reconstruction.

A second plan proposed to leave the damaged arch in its current state. However, an educational reminder of the vandals' senseless act would be constructed.

A third plan proposed the building of a replica of the arch. It would be created in a more accessible location nearby, perhaps at Lewis and Clark's campsite.

Which plan do you think is best?

QUESTIONS TO EXPLORE

- **Why is this landform called the "Eye of the Needle"?**
- **What tragic event happened to this rock formation?**
- **What plans were proposed for restoring the landmark? Which do you think is the best one?**

GLOSSARY

Bird's-eye view A view of the Earth's surface looking downward from a height.

Canyon A V-shaped valley cut by a river or stream.

Cartographer A person who makes maps.

Channel The course a stream follows; the deepest part of a river, stream, or harbor.

Compass An instrument for determining directions by means of a magnetic needle swinging freely, pointing to magnetic north.

Contour interval The distance in elevation between contour lines.

Crust The solid, rocky outer shell of the Earth.

Ecosystem A community of living things, all the nonliving things that surround it, and the relationships between them.

Elevation The vertical distance or height above sea level.

Erosion The breakdown and removal of soil and rock by water, wind, or other forces.

Estuary The wide, deep tidal mouth of a river where fresh water mixes with sea water.

Fault A break in the Earth's crust along which blocks of rock move past each other.

Fjord A long, deep, U-shaped valley inlet formed by a glacier and filled with sea water.

Flood plain Land that is covered with water during a flood, formed from sediments deposited by a river.

Geologist A person who studies the Earth and the materials of which it is made.

Gorge A narrow, deep valley with nearly vertical rocky walls.

Legend A key on a map. A legend gives explanations for the symbols on a map.

Levee A natural or artificial wall of earth material along a river or sea that keeps the land from being flooded. Artificial levees are built to control flooding.

Lock Part of a canal used to raise or lower boats between bodies of water at different elevations.

Mantle The partially molten zone inside the Earth between the crust and the core.

Map A representation, usually on a flat surface, of an area or the features of an area.

Meander A curve or loop in a river.

Moraine A mound or ridge of unsorted soil and rock deposited directly by glacial ice.

Multispectral scanner A device that senses and records data about light of different wavelengths.

Pueblo The Spanish word for "town."

Rapids Fast-moving water in a river that flows over rocks and other obstructions.

Riverbank The high ground on the side of a river.

Riverbed The bottom of a river.

Scale A ratio, fraction, or graphic ruler that shows the relationship between size on a map and size in the real world.

Sediment Tiny bits of rock, shell, dead plants, or other materials transported and deposited by wind, rain, or ice.

Source Where something comes from; its beginning.

Stratovolcano A volcano made of alternating layers of lava, ash, and other material blown out by explosive activity.

Subtropical Relating to the regions bordering the Tropics of Cancer and Capricorn.

Surveyor A person who gathers information about the sizes, shapes, and positions of land features.

Symbol An object or picture that represents something else.

Tectonic plate One of the rigid pieces of the Earth's crust.

Topographic map A map that uses contour lines to show the shape and elevation of the land.

Tributary A stream flowing into another stream or river.

Uplift A high area in the Earth's crust, produced by movement that raises the rocks, such as molten rock pushing up from below.

Water table The surface of the zone of rock, soil, or sediments that is saturated by groundwater.